you only
live ~~once~~
twice

poems by hosanna emily

You Only Live Twice

Heart Like His Publishing
Cover illustration © Isabelle Hedrick
Cover design © Josiah Chad
ISBN: 978-1-969314-00-1
Second Edition

contents

But now Christ is risen from the dead, and has become the firstfruits
of those who have fallen asleep...
The last enemy that will be destroyed is death.
...in a moment, in the twinkling of an eye, at the last trumpet. For the
trumpet will sound, and the dead will be raised incorruptible, and we
shall be changed... then shall be brought to pass the saying that is
written: "Death is swallowed up in victory."
"O Death, where is your sting?
O Hades, where is your victory?"
... But thanks be to God, who gives us the victory through our Lord
Jesus Christ.
Therefore, my beloved brethren, be steadfast, immovable, always
abounding in the work of the Lord, knowing that your labor is not in
vain in the Lord.

snippets from

1 Corinthians 15

For there is hope for a tree,
If it is cut down, that it will sprout again,
And that its tender shoots will not cease.
Though its root may grow old in the earth,
And its stump may die in the ground,
Yet at the scent of water it will bud
And bring forth branches like a plant...

If a man dies, shall he live again?
All the days of my hard service I will wait,
Till my change comes.

Job 14:7-9, 14

you only live twice

they said this life was the one i had to live...
so i groveled as a starving man
shoving pleasures in my mouth like a last meal
while every sweetness hauntingly hinted
of one less to be enjoyed.
i dug for happiness like gold,
recklessly in the rocks of "just one more."
every morsel made me hungrier,
every treasure—more impoverished
as i died a slow death in that lie.

the very trees proclaimed man's falsehood this year
as they withstood one bitter winter
and died
to live twice.

or the trunk felled which produces shoots –
daring to live again.
their skin was torn into paper
honored to write the Maker's promise:

in Me, you can live twice.

yet unlike these giants,
once resurrected
i'll never die again,
gloriously.
the One who wrote "*birth*" also penned *"rebirth"*
and *"life now"* also *"life in the Ages."*
resurrection sets me free.

i am fully satisfied, denying the appetizers of this world
for a Wedding feast is at hand.
i am the richest of souls and happier far
as i throw down my shovel, give all away,
for treasures in the heavens.
i have heard the call of, *"follow Me,"*
and i will die now
to live then
with Him.

you only live twice:

the hope of the servant today,
for that Age is far better
and Jesus—its King.

i set my gaze on that light
to traverse this curse-laden earth
for an Eden-adorned one to come.
i joy, awaiting
the revealing.

winter

*... when once the Divine longsuffering waited in the days of Noah,
while the ark was being prepared, in which a few, that is, eight souls,
were saved through water. There is also an antitype which now saves
us—baptism (not the removal of the filth of the flesh, but the answer of
a good conscience toward God), through the resurrection of Jesus
Christ, who has gone into heaven and is at the right hand of God,
angels and authorities and powers having been made subject to Him.*

1 Peter 3:20-22

winter's gentle whisper

one calendar square was a resting respite
where icy gusts died like the fall,
and winter smiled with her clear skies and sun –
warm somehow in air dreaming of snow.
the next date blew in with a torrent
of ice storms and chills in your bones,
yet both were mere blocks in a month
of thirty-one uncertain—my worrisome heart.

is it winter's gentle whispers,
or her brash, kicking screams?

every line on the calendar is blooming
into a treasure map of unknowns,
for a day is uncertain—yes,

a season more so—

yet i find rest.

the wall behind the calendar is always firm

like my King who in tenderness carried all sin on His shoulders

and came out, Victor;

Who was the Ark in a world waging flood

and preserved life for eight godly.

if that King holds my little today, He's got it.

why would i worry in winter's gentle whispers

or her brash, kicking screams?

for it is well;

i find Him, *rest for my soul.*

For I know that my Redeemer lives,
And He shall stand at last on the earth;
And after my skin is destroyed, this I know,
That in my flesh I shall see God,
Whom I shall see for myself,
And my eyes shall behold, and not another.
How my heart yearns within me!

Job 19:25-27

deciduous

i'm thankful to not be the evergreen –
for i've heard of the one who searches
to find a fountain of youth and live forever.
i'm content
to release these leaves one by one
and die a death in winter:
i know there'll be a spring.

if this body never died,
where would be resurrection?
corruption for incorruption,
death for life eternal;
not just a continuance,
but a restored body in a victorious Age to come
when death is slayed as the last enemy.

and today, in the nights growing colder,
may i take every stripping of leaves
as my God's fatherly correction
and guiding hand.

— His name is Wonderful:
"full of wonders" like resurrection, restoration, redemption —

and like a good Father, He corrects, guides me
in gentleness according to my need.
so even in brewing of winter
or winter's death itself,
i'm content being deciduous
because his name is Wonderful, and He is.

Behold, a king will reign in righteousness,
And princes will rule with justice.
A man will be as a hiding place from the wind,
And a cover from the tempest,
As rivers of water in a dry place,
As the shadow of a great rock in a weary land.

Isaiah 32:1-2

hope's song

there's darkness in this age.

the need for a hero's coming –

like frost laying siege in winter's nights,

and the roses slowly die with each one.

we don't cry because we know

spring brings resurrection every time,

but alas, this world!

she's a mother who wakes every year,

and the grave still clasps her child;

alas the heart pelted by sin's stones,

as they try to freeze and crush truth's promise.

oh, how long will this age remain,

how long winter's murderous grip?

may the faithful
– the weak, hapless sinners turned royalty by His grace –
may they ever sing hope's song:

"that a Man on that Day will be
a hiding place from the wind,
a cover from the tempest,
rivers of water in a dry place,
and the shadow of a great rock in a weary land."

my King Jesus will come, majestically:
a *hero.*
and His firelight will usher a new Age
– restoration, beauty, goodness –
and resurrection victory
in His Father's timing.

so may the faithful wait eagerly for the coming,
the pained mother hold on one more year,
until He destroys the last murderous enemy
of Death.
and the waiting will be remembered as
a very little while.

Now thanks be to God who always leads us in triumph in Christ, and through us diffuses the fragrance of His knowledge in every place.

2 Corinthians 2:14

water

the snowfall used to crush me:

a lamp, i thought, bring pummeled by icy weights,

pushing, shoving, down, down,

weight of the world.

these hands were much too weak,

and the fire in me that dared to believe

that a flame could melt winter –

my fahrenheit slowly decreased in death...

until truly warm hands took mine.

an invitation through blinding snowfall,

and He nearly carried me to a cabin just feet away

where a fire sang roaringly under a shingled roof

that could carry the sky for me.

i melted

as this Man threw wood always on the coals,

and He let my ice thaw to drip and heal on a hearth
while i read His promise above the mantle:

– *love that surpasses knowledge,*
joy inexpressible and full of glory,
peace that passes understanding –

He gave me bread and drink,
clasped my shoulder,
and said, "let's thaw this world."
so i threw open every window
and with His fire in my soul, i reentered the storm
only it didn't crush me.
the fire He put inside was a window candle
to bid the lost, "come."
though now i burn to make a change
because of the Man,
i'm indebted and in love and rejoicing
and freerer than i've ever been.
until the Day, He told me – *ecstasy unmatched* –
when spring would be brought.

every deathly flake will be water.

And I will put enmity
Between you and the woman,
And between your seed and her Seed;
He shall bruise your head,
And you shall bruise His heel.

Genesis 3:15

And the God of peace will crush Satan under your feet shortly.
The grace of our Lord Jesus Christ be with you. Amen.

Romans 16:20

what beauty

i heard that light only has definition
in the face of darkness...
and i wondered if beauty too
is only beautiful in the presence of distortion?
for i hold the dying hand of a flower kissed by frosts' poison –
loveliness wilts in the curse's winter,
melts like ice.

but it's not the death that makes life
– *life was the first* –
and so was goodness before evil,
and the lovely before mar,
forming in the fingerprints of Almighty Beauty.
all nobility is defined by the day
the Maker made something *good*,

and all today that looks like Him or His work,
that is beauty:

the healing in dirty, mechanic hands,
a waterfall thundering like heaven,
fellowship unbroken:
what true loveliness!

defying the serpent's attempts
to turn good into evil,
the Almighty will crush his head,
so we praise
and become full-time beauty seekers
in a faulty world,
giving that snake no glory.

even the Deaf sign beauty before their face,
and i wonder if it points to the comeliness of a soul created
or the unsurpassed wonder of the Beauty-Maker Himself.

... Begged Him earnestly, saying, "My little daughter lies at the point of death. Come and lay Your hands on her, that she may be healed, and she will live."

... Then He took the child by the hand, and said to her, "Talitha, cumi," which is translated, "Little girl, I say to you, arise." Immediately the girl arose and walked, for she was twelve years of age. And they were overcome with great amazement.

Mark 5:23, 41-42

healing old wounds
(talitha cumi)

You told me i am healed

from old wounds that have blistered so long,

yet i struggle to believe—

like a pup welcomed to a new family

still cowers from a shattered long ago.

help me.

these wrists remember manacles choking,

yet the prison's door remains open,

and the air never smelled fresher.

you are healed.

as You endure the ridicule to take my fingers

in freedom:

talitha cumi

a cure.
yes, i'm scared of falling again,
of hurting again;
i'm scared of being scared,
but i'm healed.

inhale,
exhale.
this freedom in Christ points to a forever one:
the Day the dead will rise,
and the tree of life will heal the nations,
but today
yes, today, i am a new creation
for Jesus did,
and He will.

teach me not to cower
but to skip like stall-fed calves
out of all prisons, powerless.
when You said, *talitha cumi,*
You meant it.
this body will die,
but it's healed, certain,

for resurrection is sure to come.

*I have fought the good fight, I have finished the race, I have kept the
faith. Finally, there is laid up for me the crown of righteousness,
which the Lord, the righteous Judge, will give to me on that Day, and
not to me only but also to all who have loved His appearing.*

2 Timothy 4:7-8

expectations

funnily, last year i learned to love running:
beginning with muscles stretching, heart pounding in anticipation,
then taking off with adrenaline speed
to settle into rhythmic breathing and focused motion.
yet a race is a battling fight
for weakness pulls at me to slow,
and i hear lies – *like every passing tree* –
pulsing in my gasping breaths and flushed face;
i resist with feet planting firmly and eyes set:

every pain pushes me closer to the Prize
so i fight on.

winter settles to ice the air in frost,
and i fight daily,

yet only grow weaker.
i learn in the everyday
strength isn't in pushing harder, like a race,
it's in the Strength Giver.
when i spring up a hill, i whisper:
this is what He trained me for.

yet when the run is over, i maybe train hardest
by waiting on the Lord, eyes set
on Him, my utter Prize,
waiting for His springtime.

He fights as i follow in submission.
Jesus is the body; i am the feet simply obeying,
and He never grows weary or slumbers,
so with His Spirit in me, why should i walk in defeat?
is there not victory in g r a c e ?

i run hard in races and will to be the feet of Jesus in today,
to achieve the ultimate Prize.
not because of my strength
– which, if i boasted in, would fall flat in the first competition –
but because of His,

         expectantly.

Therefore be patient, brethren, until the coming of the Lord. See how the farmer waits for the precious fruit of the earth, waiting patiently for it until it receives the early and latter rain. You also be patient. Establish your hearts, for the coming of the Lord is at hand.

James 5:7-8

in humble perseverance

today i saw the rarest color of a sunset
– *beyond blood-red crimson and kisses of fuchsia,*
or crowns of yellow and gems of carribean blues –
just at the hint of the horizon:

tan.
simple, pale, earth tone.
like a girl's face after a winter too long.

blushes of color crept at the edges
but were uninvited to tan's humble touch.
and it was beautiful.
in cold air the birds sang in
a sky of apricot, fair peach, skin hues
like white, but not.

hopeful tan

that didn't die in winter's curse

but trembling, takes one more breath:

spring, oh come!

tan: the remnant of color 'til Easter dawns.

and i'm the girl in winter

looking for sunshine in too-white snow

and i fight and sing and dance,

will resist the palor – *because Hope –*

until Easter.

and this girl can't wait because one sunset

– one persevering day in this cold –

will be the last

before Jesus comes again.

springtime

Restore us, O God;
Cause Your face to shine,
And we shall be saved!

Psalm 80:3

first day of spring

the first day of spring is my favorite...

and yet, it's like the sinking

of a seed into soil.

for the sun is yet to blossom,

and there's a frosty crown of icicles against stone.

i breathe in the crisp freshness of cold,

as i'm layered with unmatching jackets,

and it's spring.

a spring where birds sing,

and i sing too, despite seasonal colds,

– coughing, laughingly, utterly worship.

the greens of future flowers, buds too.

the way You turn death to life.

a springtime of *h o p e !*

one Day You'll retore this entire world like spring,

when You come in glory

like the sun destroying the clouds, but forever

and ever

and

ever.

the seed will produce a harvest,

and that's why i dance

on this first day of spring.

When I consider Your heavens, the work of Your fingers,
The moon and the stars, which You have ordained,
What is man that You are mindful of him,
And the son of man that You visit him?
For You have made him a little lower than the angels,
And You have crowned him with glory and honor.

Psalm 8:3-5

just a few inches

these filaments of pencil lead may snap or wear short

and the words written and wept over,

– if stretched to charcoal horizon –

would be just a few inches.

this life of mine,

the Gardener deems it as the flower,

which blossoms until twilight.

ahh, the delicacy of morning glory petals

which, crushed, will kiss the ground pink,

just a few inches.

and yet He plants it,

me,

delights in the words of broken pencil lead
like a Father's hand wrapped around the child's
gentle, *"let me teach you how to draw."*

and i could dance, weeping,
for He loves my offering,
and plants my blossom in His garden.
there's nothing i desire more
than to be just a few inches
with Him.

Have mercy upon me, O God,
According to Your lovingkindness;
According to the multitude of Your tender mercies,
Blot out my transgressions.
Wash me thoroughly from my iniquity,
And cleanse me from my sin.

Psalm 51:1-2

(God's Son) ... who being the brightness of His glory and the express
image of His person, and upholding all things by the word of His
power, when He had by Himself purged our sins, sat down at the right
hand of the Majesty on high,

Hebrews 1:3

simple Majesty

today, the clouds bumped like evenly-spaced bubbles
– *white cotton in near-heavenly blue* –
almost too beautiful to be real,
above my graveyard of earthly treasures.
my feet wandered a space of grass crushed
by garbage a soul deemed his all:
his livelihood in rocks and wood and bricks,
winter's dead plants,
while the celeste was nearly too lovely for words
like the curse manifested but so close to Majesty.

i saw my heart in the graveyard:
tempted to grasp worthless things
and clutter this heart with the rubbish
of selfish dreams, fears, hurts,

sins it seems i just can't release,

or my scattering of simple uselessness.

oh, may i never become a hoarder

of the treasures of this age, soon to end,

when the sun sets, and lumped clouds become peepholes

for the moon's occasional glance.

You offer Your children freedom.

may i embrace Your name as Counselor,

and, in surrender,

allow You to purge my rubbish

and make this land of my heart like Eden;

drag all away

so i am left worshipping

your simple Majesty.

holy week

Then the blind and the lame came to Him in the temple, and He healed them. But when the chief priests and scribes saw the wonderful things that He did, and the children crying out in the temple and saying, "Hosanna to the Son of David!" they were indignant and said to Him, "Do You hear what these are saying?"

And Jesus said to them, "Yes. Have you never read,

'Out of the mouth of babes and nursing infants You have perfected praise'?"

Matthew 21:14-16

Courage's entry

when they grew a house on rocky ground –

the blue sky was her ceiling,

and wind, the open windows between unsealed I-beams,

where children walked through walls, that spring.

now, doors are the only entries,

and walls are painted in beauty of tears and growth and dirty

handprints.

those years ago, other fingers held palm branches

for the entry of the most courageous Servant-Man,

as a work was incomplete,

hopelessly broken,

which only He could finish.

He was bravery incarnate,

for what courage is in the brawny arm of a sword wielder

against a defenseless enemy?

there's little valor in the boast of gods who demand

as they feast in a distant, merciless heaven,

yet tears stain my face

at the heroism of a King who leaves a throne and sword behind.

His trust is secure in His Father's plan,

and love drives Him on.

His people sang their praises

and would later slay their King, who had open arms for them.

but this spring, as the first phlox resurrect,

i sing, *"hosanna."*

we play like children do through unfinished I-beams –

for the next entry, crowned with majesty.

our King will come again, so i cry, *"hosanna:"*

– save us. –

there's tears and growth and dirty handprints of life

and a power of the very King in our souls.

while i cry at the courage-love of my Hero,

i wait eagerly with bated breath

to grab palm branches again.

You prepare a table before me in the presence of my enemies;

You anoint my head with oil;

My cup runs over.

Surely goodness and mercy shall follow me

All the days of my life;

And I will dwell in the house of the Lord

Forever.

Psalm 23:5-6

tables

oh, push over the tables of our pride,

our self-sufficiency,

– You Groom of our hearts –

so that we find ourselves sweetly at Your feet;

that's where You promise

to give us a feast at our enemy's table,

and we'll celebrate victory like the Jews on a Holy Day

with food and dance, song and jubilation,

at a future table for a Wedding feast.

And he showed me a pure river of water of life, clear as crystal, proceeding from the throne of God and of the Lamb. In the middle of its street, and on either side of the river, was the tree of life, which bore twelve fruits, each tree yielding its fruit every month. The leaves of the tree were for the healing of the nations.

Revelation 22:1-2

the Gardener

i wonder what Jesus saw
when He plodded towards a fig tree's scraggled growth
and, by His word, wilted it to the root.
did He remember the garden home He loved,
trees brimming with fruit by a Gardener's hand
and animals playing in free-style dance
under their shadows,
'til sin's darkness fell, like a threatening ax on the trunks?
or did He dream of the tree in His coming City
with different fruits every month
and life-giving leaves to heal the nations,
when He'd rule as King?

yet before, He took a tree on His shoulders
and carried it on a flesh-torn back.

the Gardener knelt under a load He accepted,
and i'm left without words.

i hunger indescribably for fruit,
and when the load looks too heavy,
i realize He carries it on His broken back
for me.

... looking unto Jesus, the author and finisher of our faith, who for the joy that was set before Him endured the cross, despising the shame, and has sat down at the right hand of the throne of God.

Hebrews 12:2

rejoice in trials

they ask me if i like to run, and i laugh.

because it hurts,

it's hard,

and i struggle behind the others under a burning sun.

but somehow

i run anyway

and tell them *yes.*

the Bible urges to rejoice in trials,

that faith tested produces a harvest of sweet patience, endurance,

i laugh at that too...

or used to.

it's hard, it hurts.

can i rejoice through silent tears?

can i dance when i run and sweat and sacrifice?

but my God does the impossible.

i read of Jesus,
how He gave thanks for the cup: His blood
and the bread: His body.
joy amidst ultimate torture, death,
struggling breaths for me.

if Jesus was the Passover lamb
i'll race through the desert sun, rejoicing,
scream my love for running, simply because
of the prize.
yes, with joy i'll enter His promised land.

For He shall grow up before Him as a tender plant,

And as a root out of dry ground.

He has no form or comeliness;

And when we see Him,

There is no beauty that we should desire Him.

He is despised and rejected by men,

A Man of sorrows and acquainted with grief.

And we hid, as it were, our faces from Him;

He was despised, and we did not esteem Him.

Isaiah 53:2-3

Man of Sorrows

i find myself attracted
– like a bee to wild goldenrod
or a photographer to mountain panoramas –
to the Man of Sorrows.

for the world says He has no form or comeliness;
i see beauty.
despised by man,
He is my treasure,
and to be in His Kingly presence is to meet utter joy
though He introduce me to His companion of sorrow.

the world hides their faces from Him and selfishly dances
to the funeral dirge of their own making.
it doesn't make sense; this paradox,

for a King to hide a treasure in an earthen box

or for me to be the finder

when His invitation is open to all.

but intimacy –

i'm adopted as a child,

and like a girl with her Protector, Friend,

i'm attracted, breathless,

in this life laid down

– His and mine –

to rise in newness, glory.

He is beautiful altogether, i know this,

and He is life,

like the pollinator's long-searched-for nectar.

Therefore humble yourselves under the mighty hand of God, that He may exalt you in due time, casting all your care upon Him, for He cares for you.

1 Peter 5:6-7

tearful surrender

i remember when You bid me surrender,

and i did.

like a Father slipping away my coloring picture,

tears fighting, i couldn't help

crying

because i love You.

but it still hurt –

useless crayons rolling from the tabletop.

now i see it.

like the bleak knife of winter slaughters

this world i knew.

all is dead and cold, bitterly

while You whisper, *hold on,*

a touch.

You use death to spring into Easter beauty:
flowers innumerable perfuming this earth
as the world's surrender brings rebirth.

the calf just minutes old with large, black eyes,
upturned nose as she wobbles to rise,
but even she came through surrender – months
of a mother's groaning, guttural labor.

within eye's reach of that blood-soaked soil,
this log i sit on,
chapped and dead, flaking away from past grandeur,
and as it rots, soil enrichens;
i already see new blossoms.

best surrender of all?
Jesus.
a King, Your beloved Son,
face of sunlit glory succumbed to sacrifice,
agony, mockery—willingly
because it too resulted in rebirth.
i'm forgiven, completely,
and Easter sings, *He rose,*
and so will i.

Father, i remember when You bid me surrender,
and i did.
my coloring picture too high on the fridge.
and as i cried, You grabbed me up,
hugging embrace, swept me into Your world
of slides and swings, awaiting, sunlit
a picnic lunch i hadn't seen You make.

and the most childlike sweetness we danced in together
began in tearful surrender.

But what things were gain to me, these I have counted loss for Christ.
Yet indeed I also count all things loss for the excellence of the
knowledge of Christ Jesus my Lord, for whom I have suffered the loss
of all things, and count them as rubbish, that I may gain Christ...

Philippians 3:7-8

(Christ) who, in the days of His flesh, when He had offered up prayers
and supplications, with vehement cries and tears to Him who was able
to save Him from death, and was heard because of His godly fear,
though He was a Son, yet He learned obedience by the things which
He suffered. And having been perfected, He became the author of
eternal salvation to all who obey Him...

Hebrews 5:7-9

not easy, but good

and when i try to define it, i make a list
of sacrifices i've made for Jesus,
of a comfort zone rejected for Him,
of long toil, hard talks, this life of dying to self.
i think of the cross You bid me carry,
and it's not easy, but good.

yet i asked a little girl, and she thought,
knees pulled up, round cheeks,
and lotion smelling of fruit loops.

"it makes me think of Jesus,"
she said, beautiful simplicity,
"'cause it wasn't easy for Him to die,
but it was good."

oh yes, a million yeses,

for any sacrifice i've made was truly a reward,

and His giving up Himself

– His gift of the cross

and resurrection life which cleansed every sin in me –

was the hardest surrender and most glorious praise.

not easy,

but so, so good.

Let God arise,

Let His enemies be scattered;

Let those also who hate Him flee before Him...

So let the wicked perish at the presence of God.

But let the righteous be glad...

Sing to God, sing praises to His name;

Extol Him who rides on the clouds,

By His name YAH,

And rejoice before Him.

Psalm 68:1, 3-4

farewells are no mistake

these tears are mystifying
for a friend who was a stranger days ago,
and now my throat chokes with goodbye.
that cautious "hello" coupled with a name,
instead of forgetting, i'll see her every time i hear it.

i don't think farewells are a mistake in Your book,
one You'll find and erase in a future;
a mar is only a blemish in the face of beauty,
and like every good story,
You'll use the brokenness to make your heroes
a happily ever after.

oh come back, Yeshua!
come, Cloud rider, and slay these goodbyes;

tears cling heavy like our last hugs
of strangers-turned-sisters.
we'll joy in Your hope
of tomorrow's epilogue
which will be all the sweeter
remembering today's goodbyes
over.

They also gave me gall for my food,
And for my thirst they gave me vinegar to drink...
Let heaven and earth praise Him,
The seas and everything that moves in them.
For God will save Zion
And build the cities of Judah,
That they may dwell there and possess it.
Also, the descendants of His servants shall inherit it,
And those who love His name shall dwell in it.

Psalm 69:21, 34-36

fragrant

this spring, i smell fragrance –

of mown grass in warm sun,

wildflowers by my feet, and distant pastures of cows,

yet i cry.

years ago on Your Good Friday,

You inhaled the vinegar smell of sour wine

and Your own blood pouring.

i know Easter is ready to bloom

but it feels as if petals are closed,

and i must watch, waiting.

faith:

those tarrying days in between.

for purpose explodes like seeds in a gale

when You said, *"it is finished,"*

and an instant pardon was the redemption of sinners;

then, Easter's beauty blossomed,

and we inhale the fragrance deeply as we wait like the disciples.

one more coming.

one more victory.

one more, *"it is finished."*

... when Your Kingdom comes.

wildflowers resurrect in spring's morning dew,

like Easter

Blessed be the God and Father of our Lord Jesus Christ, the Father of mercies and God of all comfort, who comforts us in all our tribulation, that we may be able to comfort those who are in any trouble, with the comfort with which we ourselves are comforted by God.

2 Corinthians 1:3-4

words i can't think of

my Beloved,

have you seen an artist lay crayons side by side

then apply heat, to melt in rainbow streaks,

yet block out pure paper to preserve whiteness?

ahh, remember Love,

for I see you, clutching fetal,

and you think every comfort is a word I can't think of.

rocking back and forth, your tectonic plates quake

while a hundred words of love await

for you, to still.

My heart is a love story already pouring

while your tears fall like rain on ink,

and the smudges are long and unreadable.

yet believe

they're there –

hidden under the melted crayon of your pain, shame:

while you were yet a sinner,
– ah yes, then –
before you loved Me,
before the days of your life began,
I loved.

yes, beloved, those words
– you say I can't think of –
they are already spoken over you
if you'll but take My umbrella to resist the dripping lies,
let me peel away the hardening wax of your stony heart,
and believe my Words, underneath.

may the quaking of your tectonic plates
remember that after my death
the earth quaked,
rocks split,
graves opened,
and resurrection began.

part of My love story happened
with *"it is finished:"*
paid in full.

those are some of My words of love,

but Beloved, I have so many more.

entombed

The Lord will command His lovingkindness in the daytime,
And in the night His song shall be with me—
A prayer to the God of my life.

Psalm 42:8

song  in the night

i wonder when, in darkness,

You put this song in my heart

for i awake each morning with a melody.

it wasn't there before as i fought

on my pillow with restless foes

giving every single lie

                        expectation and

                        distraction

to You with a whisper of *help me, Father.*

somehow, in the middle of twilight and dawn, the song:

victory

as i simply slept.

i could laugh when they call it just a tune stuck in my head.

Father, may i praise every morning, consistent

like the duck on the roof each sunrise,

and may Your song be the sweetness all hours

like honey oozing into shimmering, hot tea.

i'll praise and dance

– mug clasped to my chest –

(and probably spill too).

i'll sing *glory* with the angels

and wonder with the shepherds at this good news for humble me.

you awoke them with a song,

and i will join in whispered harmony

as You battle for me in the night

and give a song for the morning.

And he who does not take his cross and follow after Me is not worthy of Me.

Matthew 10:38

Take My yoke upon you and learn from Me, for I am gentle and lowly in heart, and you will find rest for your souls. For My yoke is easy and My burden is light.

Matthew 11:29-30

matthew

Father, i'm confused

as You challenge me to take up my cross and follow You

then pull me close, whisper of

rest – My burden is light.

is a cross not a weight on my shoulders,

crushing, pressing?

i crumble to the ground where spring's wildflowers are:

deadness, like winter, even in fresh soil and green ferns,

like an old log flaking away.

i sprawl.

do i do more or rest more, Father?

for i'm confused like first day of spring

that still feels like winter.

but rest is a promise and lightness too

(and You keep Your Word without fail).

so may i be one of those helicopter seeds

– blow crazily free wherever You choose –

to land, sink deep into soil's sleep,

rest as You grow this weakness of mine into an oak

simply by the strength You pulse through my roots.

like a tree, i will lift my hands in praise,

stand in You through a gale,

and scorn winter's knife

as i sleep.

i will carry my cross

because i'm in Your rest

and after winter, it'll be spring again:

You promise.

the first day of spring is a promise

like resurrection.

this dichotomy

(which is a big word for me)

i surrender to You.

if You say rest, i will, with a joy as bright as the flowers

and You'll help me carry my cross,

so i'll do that too

in resting, joyful loyalty.

simply i say

yes, Father.

And to wait for His Son from heaven, whom He raised from the dead,
even Jesus who delivers us from the wrath to come.

1 Thessalonians 1:10

brewing

i love this word that holds so much anticipation –

like coffee on a Sunday afternoon.

that moment of waiting

– sweet richness of dark grounds –

then the pouring which the brewing made true.

and that storm in the distance,

approaching thunder, blasting wind,

a bracing

or a rest.

for rain to come forth and give life.

brewing.

like today as i wait for Jesus

expectantly so,

and the returning of my Messiah King will satisfy all,

like the days His body rested,

sabbathed,

in a garden tomb,

and hope brewed, invisibly, for crestfallen disciples.

the heart tired of hope may give in.

(like instant coffee brewed in a second,

or a forecast to claim rain afar off,

in which is there fault?)

yet may it not be me, Lord!

may we wait

though it's long and so hard.

that Day is brewing.

For our citizenship is in heaven, from which we also eagerly wait for the Savior, the Lord Jesus Christ...

Philippians 3:20

where did it all go?

i stood on a wintery beach dune of a Great Lake

and couldn't help but run,

race barefoot through the sand to the spray,

and my heels were numb and ached,

but it didn't matter somehow

because Him.

He was there.

His glory in the crashing waves and beauty

indescribably near.

in this world, the cold stifles,

winter's death close and near and choking,

and i could cry daily

because i'm an engaged girl waiting

for a Wedding.

i thought once that the promise was enough,

but no,

i'm aching endlessly for the fulfillment of the promise,

the end of engagement and entrance to more.

i miss Jesus so bad it hurts,

and these moments –

the beach reminds me of the ring on my finger

because His Spirit in me dances,

and it's so like the Wedding i can imagine it.

Thus says the Lord, your Redeemer,
The Holy One of Israel:
"I am the Lord your God,
Who teaches you to profit,
Who leads you by the way you should go."

Isaiah 48:17

clearing a table

something about clearing a table
means an old moment is gone
– laughter, connection, comradeship,
a meal or coloring picture or lesson –
and i cry as i clean it and smile too
while opening space for a new moment.

Again, the kingdom of heaven is like treasure hidden in a field, which a man found and hid; and for joy over it he goes and sells all that he has and buys that field.

Matthew 13:44

remembrance

i love the first meetings:

unknowingly changing lives like sunrise's rotation,

because it did mine.

like the disciples halting at a Man who bid, *"follow Me"*

and recklessly stepped forward.

as foolish as treading waves barefoot.

but i threw my teenage heart at His soles,

tears of, *"i want to know You"*

only Him...

years slip by, and, unseen as the wind, a Friend is everything.

i've never loved Jesus more than today.

for He said, *"seek,"* then lets us find,

like a Daddy hides Easter eggs,

save He is the treasure itself.

the disciples were reckless to follow a Man
who promised food to thousands,
and i am more satisfied by a Soul i've never seen,
than this entire world,
somehow.

first meetings may blossom to the full plumage of petals
as they did for the shredded greenery of disciples' hearts
when He lay cold in a tomb,
un-beating heart,
day before Easter.
it started with a *"follow Me,"*
and we're still dancing in the continual fellowship
and holy surrender
of *"follow Me"* every day.

the prize is knowing
Him,
whose heart now pulses
                              life.

rebirth

And when Jesus had cried out with a loud voice, He said, "Father, 'into Your hands I commit My spirit.'" Having said this, He breathed His last.

Luke 23:46

... You take away their breath, they die and return to their dust. You send forth Your Spirit, they are created; And You renew the face of the earth.

Psalm 104:29-30

breathless

there is a God who breathes life into bodies of death –
like a man in the garden formed by His word
who could speak and dance and create and love
a little like his Maker.
until he decided to be more,
and sin turned the breath into shallow gasps,
and he inhales them.

this soul slowly dies,
and when the Breath Giver came, i cursed Him:
i struck the face of my High Priest
and killed my King, saying he was not.
oh, forgiveness!

this God seeped out every bit of oxygen from His lungs
in death,
– *Maker of breath letting His die* –
then life came again, like the tulips.

and i stand in another garden, in a breathless cry of *"my Lord!"*
to the One who makes my body of death come to life,
both today
and from my empty grave in an Age to Come.
i can speak and dance and create and love truly
because of my Rabboni:
the One who teaches me
and the One who gave breath
in the garden.

Purge me with hyssop, and I shall be clean;
Wash me, and I shall be whiter than snow...

Hide Your face from my sins,
And blot out all my iniquities.

Create in me a clean heart, O God,
And renew a steadfast spirit within me.

Psalm 51:7, 9-10

your hands are beautiful, Love

in the shadows, my fingernails are short, dull,
and cuticles calloused from labor i falter in, and yet
your hands are beautiful, Love.

i lift them to sunshine –
washed from the dirt of unworthiness and ineptness
in a holy beauty.
immense value
from the One who drew every crevice
to make my fingerprints:
– a lovely assortment of arches, loops, whorls –
to flow into my palms, my skin,
artwork.
your hands are beautiful, Love.

the scars and deformities

will be drowned by the fresh flooding

of resurrection

when this body will die like a seed and bloom new.

so today i lift them to the praise of His glory,

labor these palms in joy,

and tomorrow will raise them in newness:

incorruptible beauty like You, O God, my Love.

"He is not here; for He is risen, as He said. Come, see the place where the Lord lay."

... And as they went to tell His disciples, behold, Jesus met them, saying, "Rejoice!" So they came and held Him by the feet and worshiped Him.

Matthew 28:6, 9

thorns

this world brims with thorns;

i try to place my sandaled feet with care between their teeth,

yet they pierce my soles; i bleed.

the curse latches like a snake i can't shake.

child's face blooms like spring

while strangers bemoan like winter's groping fingers,

"oh, how could one bring a youth up in this age?"

can the hopeless voices not hear

Easter's songbirds and the chorus of the church?

do they not see the forests alight with wildflowers,

the mayapple opening her dual-faced leaves to diffused sun,

and the way souls drop to their knees

to bind the heel of their thrown-sliced comrade?

i dance in the thorns with my blood,

yet it's dance nonetheless.

and the pain of the crucifixion

is healed, like the cloths containing no dead body.

oh child, rejoice!

in the garden of promises, dance in our mighty King's truth!

one Day, He will gather the wheat of our hearts

and burn the thorn-laden tares with fire.

we wait for the serpent to be crushed,

and you'll bleed, child,

but our King already won once,

and in Him, we'll also have victory;

for the snake will die, undoubtably,

and He delights to fight through His young sword-wielders too.

rejoice!

In Him was life, and the life was the light of men. And the light shines in the darkness, and the darkness did not comprehend it.

John 1:4-5

lovely hands

she had lovely hands, but didn't know it:

the palms that hid under wrinkles

like a glove stretched, veins through transparent skin –

blue streaks, like ribbons of rivers that flow life.

they may have trembled as she fingered through cash

to reach out, pay for an order.

i wondered if her outstretched wrists were chained,

invisible,

when King Jesus had paid her order.

her smoker-cough raked as she turned

– that voice that was meant to sing –

and one Day maybe would again...

for her body *– her hands –* were meant

for purpose.

she was offered royalty,

wrists to be free,

and freely spread Kingdom hope like sunflower seeds

until blooming, those veined hands would change

to beauty all can see.

i saw them today

through Jesus' eyes:

lovely

because the Beautiful One both

made them Himself

and desires to embrace them as His daughter.

her hands were created for life, riant,

and Jesus declared them lovely.

i pray she would know that.

awaiting

And you yourselves be like men who wait for their master, when he will return from the wedding, that when he comes and knocks they may open to him immediately.

Luke 12:36

restless throne

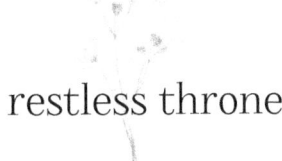

we sang of a King on a throne,

but longing creased my brow –

because it's not the throne You yearn for.

the Love of my soul is too far away,

and a long-distant engagement is the sweetest thing i know

until surpassed by Your presence

on our Wedding Day.

You are not content to linger on Your Father's throne,

not when a bride awaits, perturbed by the enemy,

not when the final throne of David seems empty in Zion,

not when the prophesies remain unfulfilled.

You hear our love-prayers,

"on earth as it is in Heaven,"

so shall it be.

be restless, my King, be restless,

and let not Your Father's throne be double-filled too long.

Your bride awaits Your coronation victory

and the seating of David's throne, complete

in Zion.

the sweetest thing ever to be known.

Therefore David blessed the Lord before all the assembly; and David
said:

"Blessed are You, Lord God of Israel, our Father, forever and ever.
Yours, O Lord, is the greatness,
The power and the glory,
The victory and the majesty;
For all that is in heaven and in earth is Yours;
Yours is the kingdom, O Lord,
And You are exalted as head over all."

1 Chronicles 29:10-11

Sky Painter of the east

my eyes gazed west as the sun rose,

and i planted trees behind my back

unknowing as my enemy handed me a trowel, gleefully,

and i wondered how the skies were so grey this morning.

they tell tales of Christian life victorious

like instagram sunrises of matchless hues.

i yearn.

i ache.

i dream and trip on reality but run in hope anyway.

the western sky contains no morning's glory

even as i tear apart clouds to search her innermost.

oh wretched girl that i am!

no matter my prowess

no sunrise graces those skies.

yet i hear of an Artist,

Sky Painter of the east
who will come one Day to adorn this whole planet
in sunrise glory.
i fall at His feet with trembling hand;
He calls my name
and turns me east to see the dawn:
the choppiest of radiance through self-planted trees!

scarlet of purifying vibrance
gold in glistening light
gentle pinks kissing the skies

a beauty beyond my imaginative years!
and there's victory
as Jesus' death is the turn to a new destination,
His perfect life in me begins to slice the forbidden trees of my
heart
so i can see.
see.
wonder of it!
the sunrise is blooming
until she opens in fullness
on that Day.

Therefore comfort each other and edify one another, just as you also are doing.

1 Thessalonians 5:11

spring is for fighting

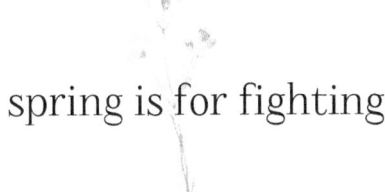

it was once said that spring was when kings went out to battle,

and the sunshine on blossomed trees

and violets smiling in forest foliage,

they make me dance...

yet fight too.

like how i'm a new creation in Christ, delightfully so,

but until He is forever light, night comes every eve',

and, with it, remnants of winter's cold.

i could be an isolated wildflower fighting the frost,

yet He gave kings their armies

and me, family:

so many new creations blooming in one woody bunch

and defying this age of cold shadows

for a new one when He returns, like summer's warmth, secure.

spring is a time for battle,
and dancing in tender grasses
for our King's victory is as certain
as if it had already happened.
so we wait.

And do this, knowing the time, that now it is high time to awake out of sleep; for now our salvation is nearer than when we first believed. The night is far spent, the day is at hand. Therefore let us cast off the works of darkness, and let us put on the armor of light.

Romans 13:11-12

at the end of the valley

soon the whole world will awake in sun's glory,

but now the earth slumbers between two mountains;

and her children cannot yet see it.

they lift an eyelid in shadows

just to sleep on.

but joy! the heart who believes

that dawn is but at the end of the valley

and for the finding.

so he rolls up his sleeping bag

and leaves the tent behind

to find life.

breath is fog,

same as a breath off the lake he travels to,

and as he waits

    and watches

he sees a shine:

where geese fly oft in black, shadowed wings,

they now reflect sun, as if transformed into a fiery Phoenyx:

dawn coming soon!

and joy for the heart who waits,

                    watches,

            and believes,

soon doused in glorious warmth.

while the world –

she slumbers unaware,

until the sun rises in justly due fire.

For I consider that the sufferings of this present time are not worthy to be compared with the glory which shall be revealed in us. For the earnest expectation of the creation eagerly waits for the revealing of the sons of God. For the creation was subjected to futility, not willingly, but because of Him who subjected it in hope; because the creation itself also will be delivered from the bondage of corruption into the glorious liberty of the children of God.

Romans 8:18-21

golden glow

i showed my sister the golden hour

when afternoon and sunset collide in earth-warming glows,

and now, she squeals with each one, delightfully.

i breathe awe too

but not just in late-day color.

my mower roars circles around the field

from burning noon to dew-laden shadows,

weaving in and out, light and dark,

and gold:

yellow on the goldenrod kissed by hot sun,

on splotches of light on a forest floor,

on warmth soaked into skin

and turning girlish cheeks rosy,

on old, creamy pages of a story well told.

life may have revolvings of shadow then light

– like golden hour between afternoon and sunset –

but there's light in the stars,

in the shaded times of life,

and always

for the disciple of Jesus,

our ending is golden too.

the prologue of this age is just the start to another

far more glorious.

But God, who is rich in mercy, because of His great love with which He loved us, even when we were dead in trespasses, made us alive together with Christ (by grace you have been saved), and raised us up together, and made us sit together in the heavenly places in Christ Jesus, that in the ages to come He might show the exceeding riches of His grace in His kindness toward us in Christ Jesus.

Ephesians 2:4-7

a flower, nurtured

if value is determined by the eye of the beholder
and worth given by the opinion of the giver,
then i am a flower
of pricelessness.

for if one of great skill recommends me
while a child taunts my worthlessness,
is my heart burdened with care?
or if my Beloved showers me with affection,
do i need the approval of another?

and so, if the whole world berates me,
if they find the work of my hand in lack,
my soul – *oh yes* – is well!
for my value was set on that Day

when God spent His Son for me
and now Himself lives each moment within
until another Day of the Wedding.

no inept valuer can sway my worth
as every work He gives me to accomplish
was hand-selected
by the Best One of All.
my Beholder and Giver's opinion matters only,
and He tenderly loves and carries me on, declaring me, us:
His own flowers
of pricelessness.

Go therefore and make disciples of all the nations, baptizing them in the name of the Father and of the Son and of the Holy Spirit, teaching them to observe all things that I have commanded you; and lo, I am with you always, even to the end of the age." Amen.

Matthew 28:19-20

next

there's always a moment after, a next,
and i hold her invitation too close,
blotting my eyes:

the next page to turn,
place to be,
the moment after i pen this poem,
the one after you read it.

she's adventure's call or monotony's curse,
a dream worth dreaming.
but between her two towns, i drove with my sister
in the not-yets, the present moment,
and we saw clouds:
a sky to study for hours and never tire

as generous lumps of white

in aura blue expanse,

and we imagined they were animals, shapes.

"a tent wide open with bushes in front!"

we laugh.

it's our calling,

in this age after Eden and before a new one:

to rejoice always.

to live thankful.

strangely, it's found in a life laid down

and a mission to, *"go and make disciples."*

it's the Gospel life.

our "next" is heavenly,

oh yes, we dream!

and joy in the nows, regardless

because He is here in today –

the Painter of the sky's cumulous, our Best Friend.

He will be in the next too –

after this poem.

after life.

and after resurrection.

Then Mary said, "Behold the maidservant of the Lord! Let it be to me according to your word..."

Luke 1:38

underfoot

somehow, a tree that's bent under storm's breath

will rise to stand victorious again;

a blade of grass pressed and trampled underfoot

though a hundred times,

will slowly unbend to reach the sun.

may i be the same:

always give of myself

and joyfully rise to praise my Maker;

see strength in the armor of humility

though the earth deems it peasant's garb.

may i now serve as a simple maidservant of the Lord

for He will later raise me up to reign as a King's daughter.

may i give and give again as the trees and the grass.

and as a drop of water tumbling always down
will laughingly sing in rain chimes,
i'll do the same, knowing and trusting my Father
for even sacrifice is a joyful gain.

If you then, being evil, know how to give good gifts to your children, how much more will your Father who is in heaven give good things to those who ask Him!

Matthew 7:11

unheeded warning

a gift today:

of cleansing rain on aggregate sidewalks

and puddles in the driveway.

i hide away from drops, and somehow there's a chorus

of a waking home, birds' happy songs, and the rain's chatter –

all one melody in crisply, cold air.

the sandbox is an ocean

dancing in every splay of drops,

and if it wasn't for this paper, maybe i could too.

rain – and birds still fly,

geese stand as if oblivious,

and every dandelion stalk is stripped.

some say the storm isn't a gift,

but i know You, Father,

my Giver.

this rain will make spring grow.

so i'll nod to the voices of *be careful,*

(but maybe be girlishly giddy)

for this gift in rainy melody

today.

That you may be sons of your Father in heaven; for He makes His sun rise on the evil and on the good, and sends rain on the just and on the unjust. For if you love those who love you, what reward have you?

Matthew 5:45-46

That at the name of Jesus every knee should bow, of those in heaven, and of those on earth, and of those under the earth, and that every tongue should confess that Jesus Christ is Lord, to the glory of God the Father.

Philippians 2:10-11

blessed by all

You cause Your sun, in dawn to rise,
a bridegroom chamber in the skies
upon the face of every man –
the evil and the good,

and how much more, to those who hate
the loving footstep of Your gait,
to them You gave Your cherished Son
to make way for His bride.

for like a flower pressed by weight,
the ones You love hide face in hate.
though Lover buried, crushed, does not
though blocked from eyes, give up.

but those who love You see His face
in risen glory, by Your grace,
and never could we hide our eyes –
on Him, our gazes feast.

and when the trumpets sing at last,
the Bridegroom from His chamber blast:
a flower dried to perfect hue
admired by them all.

the saints will dance – for Wedding dressed;
the Son of Man is crowned and blessed
by every face the sun has touched –
the evil and the good.

For then you will have your delight in the Almighty,

And lift up your face to God.

You will make your prayer to Him,

He will hear you,

And you will pay your vows.

Job 22:26-27

visiting card

i'm invited into the intimacy of Your presence

always, today, in this moment.

like a vintage visiting card

from the heir of a great plantation...

yet Your gardens are always near.

today is a more normative love,

but equally sweet

in a car tight with family, quiet in sleep,

and i see pretty town houses

which fade to fog-laden fields, dancing in sunlight.

stone bridges where birds fly

and when we drive over, the rumbling jars my pen.

i can't sit in diligent study,

but my heart is alight, a feast,

in whisper-prayers.

and if we drive to the end of the earth,

You'll be there too,

here at the West Virginia border

i joy to be a child dandled on Your knee

and when mist shoves drops up my windshield and sun is a
memory,

may You pick me up in Your arms

and strap me to Yourself as a babe

for intimacy of abiding, Your visiting card,

is the strength of my soul.

But none of these things move me; nor do I count my life dear to myself, so that I may finish my race with joy, and the ministry which I received from the Lord Jesus, to testify to the gospel of the grace of God.

Acts 20:24

silver crown

the wood-stained porch wears a silver crown

of raindrops

in that in-between moment of two storms.

lightning, the flash of gunshots,

reverberating in surround-sound thunder

– all deep beauty –

though the curse creeps like revolution's bullet.

a tear falls down the window,

and she's clean

unlike the dust-smeared glass.

may i be her.

for i am apt to lay, lifeless in puddle's dregs

when i am called to more:

grace is the power of my soul,
the ability for a drop to bring spring life
and one clean streak down a window.

while the curse wages war,
my victory-promising King is sure as crowned,
and i'm simply invited to join
as He equips me with His weapon of grace.

so fight on, storm!
there's no fear in this love.
i'll see your demise
as sure as the silver crown on my porch's floor.

Thus says the Lord who made it, the Lord who formed it to establish it (the Lord is His name): "Call to Me, and I will answer you, and show you great and mighty things, which you do not know."

Jeremiah 33:2-3

purposeful

i saw lavender skies

and the blood red of a twilight spent,

rolling, like a dream on a pillow,

to reveal the sunset continually moving westward.

i thought i missed the glory,

night yawning to swallow it up,

yet the tail end was its own beauty,

as the Maker whispered:

– *this moment I planned.* –

not the gently blue periwinkle,

the early peaches,

or hues of tangerine,

but this last, fiery beauty

which told that there's never lateness with Him.

every step,

every soul,

every love,

every jot in my story was written with purpose.

even this sunset sky about to slumber

was an invitation into

His very near presence.

Saying:

"We give You thanks, O Lord God Almighty,
The One who is and who was and who is to come,
Because You have taken Your great power and reigned.
The nations were angry, and Your wrath has come,
And the time of the dead, that they should be judged,
And that You should reward Your servants the prophets and the saints,
And those who fear Your name, small and great,
And should destroy those who destroy the earth."

Revelation 11:17-18

that Day

dear Father, i'm in the battle
between haunting darkness and transforming light,
and the age-old war zone is this earth.

for night whispers: *freedom* –
no one sees.
so i can dance and laugh and be,
but i'm surrounded by monsters,
and if i don't see my chains,
that doesn't mean they aren't there.
dancing with bonds is strangely like stumbling.

daylight is a promise,
a hope

not yet here.
like the sword in Jesus' hand on that Day
i wait for.
when every power of darkness will be slain.
even d e a t h.

so i won't succumb to the haunting
for light, true, exposes my sins
but makes me more like Him.
and even if this age is ruled by darkness
i see candle light of Jesus' Spirit
and will dance and laugh and be
in that hope.
for morning will transform this war zone
and demolish the haunting enemy.

In this is love, not that we loved God, but that He loved us and sent
His Son to be the propitiation for our sins...
And we have known and believed the love that God has for us. God is
love, and he who abides in love abides in God, and God in him.

1 John 4:10, 16

The people who walked in darkness
Have seen a great light;
Those who dwelt in the land of the shadow of death,
Upon them a light has shined.

You have multiplied the nation
And increased its joy;
They rejoice before You
According to the joy of harvest,
As men rejoice when they divide the spoil.

Isaiah 9:2-3

soft as velvet

i'm the daughter of a King, fierce

in His anger.

for light allows no shard of darkness

to tarnish His land,

yet, when these cross-forgiven feet touch the throne room carpet,

i'm immediately in His arms.

and no one else knows:

His embrace is soft as velvet.

Oh, that You would rend the heavens!
That You would come down!
That the mountains might shake at Your presence—

Isaiah 64:1

Which He worked in Christ when He raised Him from the dead and seated Him at His right hand in the heavenly places, far above all principality and power and might and dominion, and every name that is named, not only in this age but also in that which is to come.

Ephesians 1:20-21

throne above me

what utter joy has come to me –
no distant Heaven fantasy
or other world reality,
but a throne above me!

a covering has blocked its face
yet just beyond, a real-life place:
a throne room Kingdom in our space,
yes, a throne above me.

and oh, to know my prayers You hear!
You're not too far to turn Your ear,
to know You physically are near,
a throne, yes, is above me.

one Day – *i ache* – the veil will rend,
Your heav'nly armies will descend,
the Son of Man, this age to end;
You'll leave the throne above me.

and on this earth, You'll place Your throne;
the nations come to Zion, moan.
the seat of judgement is Your own,
still, a throne above me.

for i will see this earth restored,
Your children joy before You, Lord,
in healing, life, and more – *reward*
from Zion's throne above me.

that's why i will endure today:
Your prize – i'll give my life away
and pray Your Spirit lead each day;
i'll view Your throne above me.

ah, You my Friend and noble King
i love Your throne above me.

thank you:

If it appears that a writer publishes something independently with their own arsenal of talents, that is (usually) very much wrong, and I'll quickly admit that these Easter-y poems wouldn't be here if I was left to "poet" alone! I'm humbled that God gave me these pieces. I'm also humbled by the team of faith-family He provided me with.

To my huge, crazy-fun, sweet-savage family: *thank you.* You've always supported the leading of the Holy Spirit in my life, been my biggest cheerleaders, first readers, prayer group, fellow fangirls, and I'm honored to call you family!

Thank you to the early readers who joined this project through prayer, thoughtful feedback, and simple encouragement: Jubilee, Chloe, Misti, Jessica, Emmy, Erika, Abigail, Kennedy, April, Lana, Praise, Kristine, Treasure, Shira, Laurel, and Miriam, you are true blessings and "en-courage-rs"!

Izzy, I am honored that you used your God-given gift to grace the book cover! Thank you for your sisterhood in the Gospel! And Josiah, thank you for your formatting, text, and graphic work and for your song "Travel On," through which God taught me the truth that we get to live twice. ;) You both serve our Messiah freely, and that inspires me.

To Laurel who hosted a holy-week poetry challenge which God used to spark the idea for this book—thank you, girly! Your Kingdom poetry and heart of encouragement is *beautiful.* And I wouldn't be surprised if your own lovely poem "You Only Live Twice" is partly what God used to inspire the title. <3 Thanks for so much.

To my dear Father, the Love of my Soul, and my Best of Friends, thank You for writing the story of Easter with Your own blood. The life I have in You is the happiest thing I know! Thank You for every poem. I pray they display even a tiny portion of Your immense beauty.

shalom,

hosanna emily

about the poet

Because of the grace of God, Hosanna Emily is a warrior poet: a warrior because God is her Father (which makes her a crazy-in-love princess) and she lives fighting to be faithful for the day Jesus' Kingdom will come and a poet because she loves beautiful, truth-filled words. Thus, she fills her journal with poetry, her blog with urges to live for Jesus, and then writes books on top of that—from fantasy to middle grade and more—stories to inspire radical living for the coming King who is worthy.

On a normal day, you may find her homemaking on the family farm, going on long walks, singing worship, cooking healthy food, playing Frisbee, randomly dancing the Virginia Reel, dreaming of Jesus' coming Kingdom, and enjoying life with her family of more than a dozen amazing people and her Church family of even more.

hosannaemily.com
havingaheartlikehis.blogspot.com
Instagram: *@hosanna.emily*

a war is waging, and a King is coming.
thus, these poems sing.
they utter war-cries of faith for the one thick in battle.
they whisper teardrops of hope for the aching soul.
and they overflow in dancing, giggling worship because of love.
in stories and colors, emotions and beauties,
they're an anthology drawing together to testify of the King
through heartfelt moments and
genuine truth
and in free verse and rhyme and behind-the-scenes stories.
an arsenal of indie artists are featured within their pages,
and laughingly, these more than eighty poems sing of joys to come
(like a poem with giraffes).
may every word
stir one's heart to live for that Kingdom.

available on amazon